GEDICHTE

by Mary-Katherine S. Kraeger
The Farmer's Daughter!

Averlune Press, Inc.

Averlune Press, Inc.
www.averlune.com

Publisher's Note: This is a work of poetic fiction. Names, characters, places, and incidents are a product of the author's imagination. Locales and public names are sometimes used for atmospheric purposes. Any resemblance to actual people, living or dead, or to businesses, companies, events, institutions, or locales is completely coincidental.

Dedication: This book of poetry is dedicated to my parents. To my Mom, who taught me to read and write, introduced me to literature and always encouraged me to try anything. I love you just the way you are!! To my Dad, who was always there to read anything I had written and listen to me talk through any idea whether it made sense or not. I miss you more than I can say!!

1. POETRY / All

ISBN/SKU: 9798218079895
ISBN Complete: 979-8-218-07989-5
Publication Date: 12/09/2024

Gedichte/Mary-Katherine S. Kraeger. -- 1st ed.
ISBN 979-8-218-07989-5

This book of poetry is dedicated to my parents.

To my Mom, who taught me to read and write, introduced me to literature and always encouraged me to try anything. I love you just the way you are!!

To my Dad, who was always there to read anything I had written and listen to me talk through any idea whether it made sense or not. I miss you more than I can say!!

Thanks to Miss Clare, for editing, and Uncle Matt, for all his help and advice.

This book of poetry is dedicated to my people.

Table of Contents

Introduction

Poets, artists, musicians, and *penseurs* of every persuasion have, since time out of mind, been trying to capture by means of clumsy mediums what only the heart can apprehend. There are few pursuits more futile than these, and no futility quite as essential to the enrichment of the human experience.

But it's not simply enrichment that we seek by means of such pursuits as the penning of poetry. It is a deeper and more profound *expression* of our shared experience. It isn't enough to think and feel and experience life, we are compelled to speak life, too.

While, it is true, that the subject matter of poetry is often the specifically personal experiences of the poet, these experiences can be therapeutically relatable. In other words, poetry is universal.

Within the pages of this collection of poems, Mary-Kate describes with innocence and insight universal themes in a manner that both enriches and gives expression to our common experience of life.

I urge you to read these poems with an openness to the goodness, truth, and beauty which are the kernel and purpose of every moment. I am certain that the author's perspective will enrich and enlighten your own. Enjoy!

Matt Pelicano
Poet & Author

POETRY

Snow

After tree leaves turn colors and fall
After geese fly south answering a call.
Before grass pokes through the muddy ground
And dandelions bloom on pitchers' mound.
Flakes come falling from heaven
Lighter than bread that is unleavened.
Forming a layer of glistening white
Cold air and snow descend overnight.
Covering trees, bushes, houses, and cars.
Coming from the clouds that hide the stars.
Skiing, sledding, ice-skating, many sports.
Snowballs fights in and around snow forts.
Enjoying the snow every free day.
Playing with others in the warm sun's rays
Through the winter months our souls will soar.
Until all the piles of snow are no more.

Breeze

Wafting, cruising,
Dancing away.
Absorbing, ambling,
Along its merry way.

Charming, face-lifting,
Creating a break.
Growing, dying,
Asleep, awake.

Nudging, nestling,
Very drowsily.
Playing, alluring,
Rather moodily.

Singing and walking,
Oh, so daintily.
Soothing gently
Quiet; a water lily.

Swooping, tantalizing,
Mysteries on the air.
Uplifting, down pouring,
Tasting everyone's affairs.

Lifting and wending.

Waxing and waning.
Unveiling yearnings.
Almost unending.

Whispering everything.
Teaming with feelings
Stilling, moving.
Finally vanishing.

Summertime

Blue skies, warm and sunny
white clouds drifting by
Breezes blowing in the trees and across the fields
birds chirping and bees humming
Half-naked sandy little boys
Dozing dogs, and scratching chickens
Laundry flapping on the line
Machinery waiting to be fixed
Hay in the fields drying
Farmers sweating while at work
Unloading load after load
Stacking hay in a hot barn
Music playing, people partying
Bonfires and late nights
Hamburgers, hot dogs, and cold drinks
Fireworks and fireflies lighting up the night
Summertime full of myriads of things
Old and young living their lives
Everything not always as we would want
But we are easily preoccupied
And make new memories
To enjoy all winter long.

POETRY

Snow in the air

Winter breeze twirling
snow around and around
up and down softly
it falls and rests.
Weak pale sun
sheds little warmth
to the earth
to melt the snow.

Corn

Pile of fresh ears,
crispy green outside,
soft yellow and white kernels beneath,
silk soft and slippery.

The smell of propane and corn,
mixing with the sound of flies and dogs,
The feel of the rubbery kernels,
the "RIPP" of shucks being peeled off.

Bobbing in hot water on the grill,
chilling in the cold tub,
cut up into tasty golden piles,
to fill little bags with farmers gold.

Piles of shucks and cobs,
bed and breakfast for the pigs,
winter meals in the freezer,
fresh butter and sugar corn!!!

Storming

Before the storm blows in.
A quiet calm descends.
The humidity and heat rise.
And the darkening clouds approach.

Then, at first,
As closer it moves.
You hear the distant thunder sound
And you feel the wind grow strong.

Then a crash of thunder!
A flash of lightning!
A sheet of rain descending!
A roaring wind blowing!

A crash of thunder sounds,
Like a hammer on an anvil!
A flash of lightning lights up the sky,
Like firework on display.

The rain falls.
A constant stream from the sky.
The wind blows hard,
Moving everything in its path.

The storm continues

With all its might.
Blocking out sight of the moon.
Raging thru the night.

After it passes
All you hear
Is the far-off roll of thunder
And the drip-drip of water in the trees.

Then there is calm
A cooling sense of relief
The storm is gone.
The land and sky are at peace.

End of Day

Nighttime is falling,
Clouds are drifting by,
Stars are twinkling up above,
All thru the night.

People sleeping,
Breezes blowing,
Peace around us,
Slowly descends.

Moon is hovering,
Leaves are fluttering,
Children dreaming,
As they slumber.

Animals abed,
The world is quiet,
Streetlamps flicker,
In the darkness.

One Autumn Night

I saw seven shooting stars that night as we sat
around a bright campfire,
we stared up at the star filled sky, each one twinkling,
each one gleaming.
We roasted 'mallows and talked of cars and days gone by.
As coy dogs and beagles sang in the background,
the wind rustled through autumn-colored trees,
and the tarp that covered the woodpile.
We passed the cup around and sipped the wine.
Oh, how the hours, days, and years rush by us:
we grow old,
in body and in mind.
We should make more time to do things like this,
but in stark reality we know that we will not be able to,
and we will be left with memories warm like the fires glow,
even to the day when we lie cold like the darkness outside
the fire's ring!

HNROV *(smile)*

Curved (beak)
Hyperbolic (drama)
Interesting (attitude)
Colorful (feathers)
Kingly (baring)
Entertaining (funny)
Noisy (cluck)
Sassy (bird)

Wind

Blowing, chilling,
Crying shrilly.
Pushing, shoving,
Moving busily.

Rushing, Tumbling,
Moving clumsily.
Hitting, Biting,
Shouting lustily.

Baffling, pelting,
Moving speedily.
Curdling, cunning,
Moving voluntarily.

Clinging, flowing,
Screaming, singing.
Growing, mellowing,
And finally ending.

Autumn

Feel the wind whip your cheek,
And chill your fingers and nose.
The sun is casting a bright glow,
Warming your face as you walk.
The rain is cold and drippy,
Covering everything with a wet spray.
The mornings are cold and crisp,
Everything hidden by the morning mist.
The tree leaves change and fall,
Drifting to sit on the ground in piles.
Squirrels and chipmunks race to store their nuts.
Deer and turkeys constantly graze, preparing for the winter.
Farmers and gardeners harvest their crops.
Silos and barns are filled; garden produce is preserved
Kitchen shelves and pantry bins are overflowing;
With tasty treats, apples, pumpkins, and drying herbs.
Wood is chopped and stacked.
Warm coats, blankets and shoes are brought out to air.
Everything is prepared for the winter ahead.
Time seems to hang suspended
As the change in the season comes about.

A Wish

Wish I was a bird
flying all around.
My spirit would be so light
I'd never touch the ground.

Wish I was a bird
With a pair of lovely wings.
With my little song
I'd let the world ring.

Wish I was a bird
With feathers of blue
and my beak a cheerful yellow
I would fly and see the view.

Wish I was a bird
Heralding the start of spring.
Making people smile and laugh
when they hear me sing.

Wish I was a bird
not sowing, nor reaping.
Feeling the wind in my feathers,
sunlight off my back leaping.

Wish I was a bird

Sitting high in a tree
So I could enjoy
Seeing all that I could see.

Wish I was a bird
I'd fly around the world
South, North, East, and West
Oh! I'd see the world

Wish I was a bird
From beginning to end,
not missing what is past,
with nature as my friend.

Wish I was a bird
I'd fly, and fly, and fly.
I'd leave all troubles and cares behind,
And fly until I die.

One View of Winter

Oh, that cruel fiend wint'r, that from my heart
Doth seem to steal away the very warmth.
Whose stormy clouds darken mine eyes and soul.
Whose days are void of triumph, and of joy,
That steer every dream into despair.
Falling snow doth promise numb face and limbs.
Chattering teeth ring in the frosty air.
Cold and piercing winds send a body bent
Rushing for heat, cover, comfort, and home.
Fields drifted with snow lie lifeless and bleak.
Trees hung with ice, stand stark, foreboding, grim,
Along the paths. Months of cold entrap us.
Yet 'neath the cold harsh ground, so silently;
Hope lies amply, waiting for springs bright sun.

POETRY

Relaxing

Floating between
earth and sky
watching the clouds
slowly roll on by.
Birds are singing
amongst rustling leaves,
evening tide descends
on everything around me.
A brisk cool breeze
recharges the body,
and gives the soul
strength to keep on

Sounds

The quiet of a forest glade.
The hum of city life.
The sounds that God has made.
The bustle of a farmer's wife.

The crooning of a mother to her child.
The singing of a maiden meek and mild.
The hum of classroom learning.
The cry of a heart yearning.

Thunder in the hills.
Quiet on the plains.
An animal's call to its kill.
The steady beat of rain.

Water trickling down, down.
The wild wind in the night.
The antics of a smiling clown.
People working and moving with all their might.

The sound of an angry storm.
The hum of a summer night.
The wind rustling in the corn.
The melee of a fight.

All these and more.

Sounds impossible to ignore.
Strike thee to the core.
And stay in your heart evermore.

Hope

The sun rises
After a stormy night
and spreads hope
with each ray of light
as gray clouds clear
and rain drops cease
the wind dies down
the world is at peace.

The Snowman

There he stands
with piercing eyes
the blue gray of gravel.
Long nose fitted
to a pale white face;
a sharp contrast
to his round fat head.
His jovial smile crookedly etched
across his frosty countenance,
His knit scarf of green and red
knotted firmly around his thick neck,
whips about in the chilly wind.
Mismatched black buttons straying
haphazardly down his middle,
betray an ample girth.
Checkered mittens shelter
crooked fingers.
Thin arms branch out
in a friendly embrace.
An old, tattered hat sits
tilted atop his bald crown
completing his quaint ensemble.
He offers a welcoming smile
and a wish for good health and joy.
Waiting in the wintry weather,
alone, except for the birds

and blowing snow.
A whisk broom, long used
stands upright in his grasp.
Covered with new snowflakes.
He stares back.

POETRY

Misty Morning

The clouds descend
to meet the mountaintops.
small cool water droplets
suspended midair.
an opaque wall
concealing our surroundings
obstructing our path.
throwing up barriers
seemingly impenetrable.

Fall

Time for sweaters,
Hats, and scarves.
Morning chills turn
to afternoon warmth.
Dying sunlight shines
through yellow, orange,
and red leaves
onto the earth.
Ready to be preserved
Fruits, grain, and seeds:
a promise for the future.
Squirrels race to fills their hoard.
Storm clouds lie on the horizon,
Hints of frost in the air.
Cozy bonfires and hot soup,
Crisp and juicy fruit.
Cobwebs stretched between
brown cornstalks.
Secrets whispered on the breeze.
Hay bales stacked in barn lofts.
Morning fog shrouds the trees.
Falling leaves lazily float in the air.
The Autumnal Equinox approaches.
Chestnuts fall, pumpkins are carved
corn mazes full of laughter
Ice-cream atop fresh apple pie

cups of hot cider and tea
ward of the descending chill.
Blessings abound.

Thoughts While Driving

Mist hangs in the air
Thick and wet
Lurking shapes arise
Sounds are muffled
Haloed headlights suddenly appear
White churches and red barns
Split rail fences covered in moss
Brown weeds line the ditch
Rain drops on the windows
Wiped away to clear my sight
Lonesome travels along
Tennessee back roads

Barnyard Breakout

A cow, a pig, and a chicken too,
squawked, and oinked, and mooed.
Their quarters were tight and smelled of poo.
Oh! what on earth were they to do.
They argued and they fought,
rapidly becoming distraught.
At their awful plight, to escape;
Yes, but not get caught.
They began to scheme:
Across the road and a fence
lay a corn field so immense
with tempting fruit so nearby:
hanging, golden and dense.
The mood quickly grew intense
so, with a mighty kick, wham!
The boards broke loose, Bam!
Quickly they took their leave
away from farm and farmer, Scram!
To live wild and free on the lam!

Colors of Nature

I wish I could paint the sky
with shades of blue and grey and white
and add the yellow fiery sun
with bright and shining rays.
I wish I could draw the grass
in diverse hues of green.
Shaded by leaves of various sizes
reaching towards heaven as they grow.
I wish I could sketch the trees
with trunks, branches, and twigs,
dressed according to each season
scattered in every direction.

POETRY

A Storm's Approach

The wind moans and wails
around roofs and trees.
It blows, scattering leaves, shaking branches.
Sends travelers hurrying along
whipped by its cold fingers.
Grey skies threaten rain
predictions of foul weather.
Inside, a deceitful calm lies,
where warmth and light pervade.
Till chatter and passing footsteps
the stillness disturbs.

A Winter Scene

Snow is falling fast
blown down on artic air.
A pity it rarely lasts.
A frenzy of white flakes
covering the land in its path.
Leafy branches evergreen
bow under increasing weight
Yards and playgrounds alike
vacant, white crystals accumulating.
Sidewalks bare of traffic
while people keep warm at home.
Snow encrusted cars creep
down wet slushy roads.
Their occupants venturing forth
as the storm dies,
As the sun rises behold
A world reborn
washed clean and white.

It's Time Again

Sun shining in a clear blue sky.
Leaves changing color, rattling, falling,
Flying in the breeze.
The last summer flowers, stand,
bent with age, petals almost gone.
Black Eyed Susan's, Sunflowers, and Mums
fill the air with their fragrance.
Yellow curbs, signs, and school busses
contrast with green shrubs and lawns.
Students chat as they stroll to class.
Cows gaze in roadside pastures,
farmers hurry to preserve corn and hay.
Fresh ground, plowed, sits, drying in the sun.
Birds chatter, flags flap, cars zoom.
The air is full of sounds and smells.
Dry leaves, ripe fruit, crisp cool air.

POETRY

Summer Sights

Red Robins fly around
White clouds float by
Blue sky stretches
horizon to horizon
Green leaves rustle
Brown dirt is our floor
Yellow sunlight
over everything

Outdoors

I wonder why I like the outdoors
why does it call to me all the time?
How I love the sky in all its shades
blue, gray, white, red, orange,
yellow, purple, and pink;
clear and cloudy, day and night.
The sun shines, giving us hope.
The moon glimmers as it travels
across the sky.
Stars sparkle and shine
telling of all they've seen.
The earth a smorgasbord of textures,
smells, sounds, sights.
Too many to catalogue.
The wind calls and sighs,
frolicking across the land,
wandering into nooks and crannies,
changing speed and direction willy nilly.
Birds, bees, fish, cattle
call home the forest, plains,
lakes, streams, deserts, and mountains.
Our wonderful natural world
loved by many, neglected by far, far more.

POETRY

Thoughts on Looking Down the Train Tracks

Nothing is as straight
as a railroad track
disappearing into the distance
a distinct silhouette of steel
cold, alien, surrounded by nature
transversing the changing landscape.

A Snowstorm

It is snowing!!
What a wonderful sight!
Though it brings dicey travel
and moments of fright.
Each falling flake
is different and yet, the same.
Brightening each daybreak
with thoughts of hope, dispelling pain.
Covering up and slowly transforming
layer by layer
natures bare form.
Each crystal a prayer,
a wish for the future,
and a brand-new day.
To act like a suture,
a healing ray.
Conjuring memories
happy and sad,
of past flurries;
of what we've had.

The sight of that first flake
gives my heart new life.
Helps me fight the sadness
the frustration, the confusion.
It keeps me going
one day at a time.

Taking a Walk

A long dusty path I traveled
straight.
Following the way of trains
long gone.
Cicada's singing in the air
loudly.
An oppressive humid tension, crackling
surrounds us.
Panting dog keeps on walking,
sniffling.
Sweat drips down faces shaded by
tree leaves.
Gunshots sound in the distance
echoing.
Powerlines and trimmed hedges on
two sides.

End of Summer

Early leaves
Fall in arcs of orange
red and yellow.
A sea of purple and green
extends over the rolling hills.
The trickle of water is heard
in the valley below.
Creek beds team with
birds and winged bugs
searching for food.
The chatter of squirrel
chasing each other
echoes alongside birdsong.

Treasure

Around the mound
colored birdseed
I gladly found
a spark of hope
scattered lightly-around
of spring ahead
on the snowy ground.

Feeding the Birds

Seeds raining down the sides,
like spring it calls
to the winged beasts
and elicits from them
a merry song.

Chirps of thanks,
appreciation shown,
as they flock around
the wood and plastic dish
hung mid-air for them.

Lines for K.

Do not get your hopes too high
until at least another month has gone by
And when you see small flowers grow
It will soon be spring, and you will know
winter will have passed on by.
The migrating birds North will fly.
Snow will thaw and water flow,
warm breezes will begin to blow.
so, smile and wait
and soon you'll see
on another date
that spring it will finally be.

Burning Cardboard on a Winter Day

I stand and feed
the voracious beast
and watch as smoke curls
and spews from every crack
and hole in the corrugated material.
Its orange claws reaching up
to pull the pile down
turning everything to black.
The only sounds are a roar
from the snarling teeth of flame,
the crackling and popping,
the drip of melting snow,
the sizzle as it hits the flames.
A mammoth consuming all it can reach.
I feel cold all but my face.
The smell of charred paper,
of hot rusty metal
hangs in the freezing air
carried away slowly.
As I leave, the job completed
the monster's mouth is gaping wide
empty as before
asking... for more.

POETRY

Early Morning

Driving into the sun,
past houses, farms, and fields.
Residents stir, in the cool air,
exiting warm homes.
School buses prowl,
clothed in bright yellow,
waiting students their prey.

Moments

Pause a second now
And listen to each sound,
And watch intensely, how
The world keeps flying by.

Look to the morning breaking over the hills,
the sun setting in the west.
The night wind rustling through the trees,
and evening animals at rest.

Hear the bird songs in the morning
And the quiet of the dark night.
The animals and the sighing trees;
the busy bees in flight.

Watch the wind gently blow
on a lovely spring morning.
The rustling leaves,
and birds a wing soaring.

See a landscape in each season's glory
covered with snow all glittery white.
With growing and blossoming flora
beautiful, quiet; my soul's delight

Study a storm in its power and wonder.

A sea sending wave upon wave.
A darkened prairie as night descends
A bright rainbow, a promise to save.

Hear, see, and feel God's love and power
Stop and experience each moment in time;
in every minute, in every hour
Throughout the ever-flowing year.

Day's End

Darkness descends
It is time to go,
a hug and kiss goodbye,
a promise till tomorrow.
The car engine rumbles to life,
lights on to brighten the way,
music playing soft and smooth.
Out from the town
past the sleeping farm
down a small hill
around the shadowed bend.
Making my way
homeward at last.
To the side, a buck
standing motionless, staring.
Unsure whether to brave the open road
or retreat to the woods.
Lights ahead mark scattered towns,
while a clear sky shows the moon rise.
Passing cars with bright light
zoom on by highlighting
power lines and road signs.
Almost there, one turn more,
two curves and down the final hill.
Home sweet home lies just ahead.
Pulling into the driveway… to finally stop.

The Stinky Afterlife

Raspberry pies and chocolate cake
And white lasagna too
All smelled delicious once.
Meat balls with sizzling grease.
Macaroni and cheese baked to perfection.
Meals to feed the masses,
these and diverse more.
Aromas arise all at once
discordant and caustic.
Smoky remnants of their former glory
incinerated into powdery ghosts
by the self-cleaning oven.

On My Way to Work

Stopped by the roadside
on a snowy Monday morning.
Listening to Sentimental Journey
my eyes wander of the glistening landscape.
Contemplating the past
and yearning for tomorrow.
Thoughts rising upwards
with the steam from my hood.
Cars pass on by
moving ever onwards.
Soon I will join the queue
unable to stop or stay too long.
Roofs drip in the warmth,
as the sun shines in a clear sky.
Winter will not last forever
the seasons ever change.
The snow and grime will fade
gone with winter's cold.
Washed clean with rain showers
Spring slowly creeps in.
The earth will blossom
new growth will abound.
A slow and steady march
Season after season.

Ode to Joy

Over sleepy mountain peaks
the sun's blinding rays.
To rise and shine below
and start a brand-new day.
Across the streets and houses
it gradually spreads and grows.
Over the awakening land
it trickles and it flows.
Golden beams alight
on everything in view.
Sending away the shadows
drying the morning dew.
Oh! What a sight,
God's wondrous creation.
A blaze with a new day's light
prompting humble oration.

Observe

The dying summer sun
slowly descending.
Shadows follow, drifting in
on cool fall breezes.
Tucked snuggly indoors
people stay, avoiding
the dark chilly night.
Stars remain hidden
behind oncoming winter storm clouds.
Squirrels scurry to hoard and save.
Trees drop colored leaves
one by one.
Lights are dimmed.
Doors and curtains closed.
The world draws inward
at the end of each day.
Yet... under streetlamps
walks a stranger alone.

THE END